BORAH's! PITIFUL POEMS & PICTURES

POEMS BY
BORAH! BREWINGTON
SNAGGLETOOTH XIII

ILLUSTRATIONS & ARTWORK BY

ZOMBIEDOG43

ALL HALLOWS EVE

Bats fly high in the dark, deep sky.
The silver-slicked moon shines dull and
bright.
Leaves whirl and swoop, in the cold,
damp air.
With the smell of all Hallow's Eve
everywhere.
Footsteps far you hear and then you
shriek.

IMMORTAL?

Dark, chilly night, now's the time

Shovel, gloves with lots of grime

Rusty lantern dimly lit, slightly show just a bit

the path is hard to see as clouds cover me

Shhhhh squeaky lantern not so loud

Dig, shruuump dig, shruuump tap tap bang

Pull it out, dust it off and haul it home to castle's lair

Hold your breath and pry the lid

squeak squeak thunk.... Look inside, it's all dead

An arm from him a toe from her a hand from him a leg from her

Stitch and sew add some fur, stitch and sew a pant, a shirt

on the slab all wired up... Raise this dead to the roof

Igor thrilled as he cranks, raising slab to the sky

Tesla bright with thin loud lights

Back and forth forth and back louder smelly almost done

Thunder cracks lighting strikes smoke a rise and all a hush

Chains pulled down towards the ground

clickety clack, clickety clack

Slab of monster, man or beast

Step back....watch, hold your breath, it no longer rests in peace

Wait....watch....wait....watch....waaaiiiiit....

frozen silence waiting....wondering....hoping....scared

Are we all prepared, a finger bends, then all five......yes yes yes IT'S ALIVE!

CANDY CORN

Oh so old as tradition goes,
yellow, orange and white,
which part do you first bite?
Is it yellow or white, such a delight.
Squeeze the orange and roll around
like a pumpkin on frosted ground.

I REMEMBER

Cold, wet, smooth plastic against my face.
My tongue pushes through the small slit space.
Thin, round elastic helps disguise me.
The pic of my costume looks nothing I'm to be.
But, we had quite a fun-filled night, didn't we?
Grabbing candy left and right,
goodbye you dented, chalky front.
Back in the box till next Halloween spree.

COMPANION

Hop on my magic broom and

arch your back while we fly

scampering past the full, fat moon...

zoom, zoom we go up and down and all around

you know how to ride a broom,

I've no worries you may fall

it's all in the fur and thick dark paws

black as soot and razor nails

hold on tight we'll fly the night

don't lose your tail

hold on tight with all your might

while I cast a spell on this night of hell

HEADLESS HORSEMAN

That Ichabod, he's tall, smart and not fancy at all.

He teaches and eats and has long clumsy feet.

He stays here and there and dances around the square.

He has a crush on Katrina Van Tassel,who's house is big as a castle.

She lives on a farm with crops healthy and tall.

She has an admirer who thinks she's just so neat.

His name is Brom Bones and has muscles from head to feet.

Tonight, Tarrytown is hopin' a trot,

there's a party that ends at 12 o'clock.

But before the strike of midnight, Ichabod, Brom, Katrina

and the gang tell tales of spooky and scary hoots.

Brom was mad thinking he'd been had,

for Katrina had her eye on the tall Ichabod.

The dark cold night drew to a stop.

Ichabod hopped on his borrowed horse, Gunpowder...

This sad worn horse was tired and had no giddy-up.

Dragging along the black, cold path out of nowhere here came the tale!

Larger than nightmares was a beastly tall man on a huge black horse casting a spell.

This beast sat and on his shoulders no head at all.

In hand were leather reins and the other a fat, round orange pumpkin.

It glew fire from its mouth, nose and glaring eyes.

It was whirled through the wet, chilly air and crashed against Ichabod's head.

When he woke it was no joke, he skedaddle and left Sleepy Hollow on the morrow.

He made sure that thing wouldn't follow, he left no trace of himself.

The whole town woke and were besides themselves, for Ichabod was nowhere to be found.

They searched high and low and rummaged the grounds. Why did Ichabod flee?

One person laughed, and asked, "Was it old Braum who could have chased Ichabod away?"

Braum thought to himself they'll never know... but will always wonder that it could've been me that made him flee.

<u>NO MOE!</u>

Candles in windows all aglow.

Kids giggle, knocking at the doe.

They say Trick-or-Treat, give me a little moe.

Back and forth I go, go, go….

Now it's over, gonna soak my feet, they soe.

<u>AFRAID I AM</u>

Mischief those kids are...
Up to no good they are...
Porch light off.
Door locked tight.
Go away!
I've no candy...
...OFF and good night!

PUMPKIN CARVING

Round, orange, sometimes textured and stemmed...

The symbol of Halloween.

Stab, saw, circular motion, pull open and ummmm...

The smell of Halloween.

Scoop, scrape, pull and hull...

The sounds of Halloween.

Separate seeds and smush the guts...

The thought of Halloween.

Carve triangular eyes, a nose and a jagged grin...

A tradition on Halloween.

Roast the seeds and spice them up...

they'll be delicious on Halloween.

Drop in a candle, light it up and close its lid,

burn every night...

Till Halloween.

<u>OURS</u>

You say it's not a holiday
but we claim it as our way.
Not only do we claim the day,
we claim October all the way!
MAN we hate it when it's over.
It's not that we condemn your views,
you can do what you choose.
So as the same,
we'll be jolly, gay and spread our news
that we look forward to our 31 days of boos.

<u>GHOST</u>

Dark dark dark inside the old wood
house
creaks and moans of every tone
a cat, a mouse, spider webs and
broken windows
shutters falling, roof sinking
......it must be...... the old man's finally
gone

<u>SALEM</u>

There's a small quaint town

stone streets abound

it borders a body of water

with ghosts on every corner

at night the sky is deep

with cemeteries on every street

where "witches" were hanged

a stubborn pressed

here Pagans, Wiccans and souls unrest

filled with spooks and fun just for you

for Salem, nothings left behind

you'll see and experience things you've never thought

be sure to come in costume

Salem means Shalom which is harmony and peace

so come along and join us in our afternoon of feast

THEY OWN THE NIGHT

Witches and Warlocks haunt the night.
Brewing their cauldrons in hopes to fright.
We sneak through the forest for a spooky
peek.
Quiet now or they'll see you if you eeeeek!

MY CHILDHOOD WAS THE BEST

The Great Pumpkin we watched forever
We'd be thrilled all together
I remember
Hoping Lucy wouldn't fool Charlie
for that football prank was gnarly
I remember
Feeling sorry for ole' Charlie
His friends treated him like poopie
I remember
Snoopy being a jerk to Woodstock
and wishing he'd just stop
I remember
Peppermint Patty being manly
knowing she'd never fall for Stanley
I remember
Linus in that pumpkin patch
hoping the Great would come back
I remember
All he got were rocks
I can relate, for Christmas, all I got were socks
Thankfully I remember
but I wish I could turn back the clock
and relive my youth before I drop

TOMB SWEET TOMB

Cold, quiet and damp
smelly, tight and cramped
spiders, worms and lots of germs
no room to move or squirm
my finger has a ring, tied to a string
I pull the bell, scream and yell
all I hear is silence, thank goodness, up there,
there's too much violence
I guess I'm doomed, I'll make myself at home
cause now, this is tomb sweet tomb

RIDDING WARTS

Grab one of those slippery, tiny green, spring frogs.
Don't squeeze it too, too hard!
Say "Hello little froggy".
Oh, make sure you do this one night when it's foggy.
Hold it in your right hand and flip it over twice and
once again.
Rub it's back 4 times counter clockwise on your wart.
Then hold it by its hind legs.
... he'll be a good sport.
Kiss the tip of your left pinkie.
Touch its belly with that finger.
That froggy doesn't want to linger....
So say goodbye to him or her, it has feelings too.
Set it free, as it hops away, tell it how much you love
thee.

TRADITION

I love to decorate for Halloween,
it's one of my favorite things.
I learned as a kid, it's just what my family did.
Starting early was pounded into my head.
It was done every year,
we started a month ahead.
We enjoyed the decorations that whole month
It was a mission that became a tradition.

<u>CEMETERY</u>

Mossy gray hanging thick and long.
Strung from limb to limb and full of stench.
When I pulled you apart, it wasn't long.
Til those red bugs caused an itch
down there on my ding dong.

<u>YARD</u>

I love to decorate for Halloween.
For Halloween is one of my favorite things.
It's not hard to decorate your yard for Halloween.
Better yet turn the yard into a haunt.
Trick or Treaters for sure would take a tour.
Attach a rope from roof to tree, fly a ghost with a pulley.
Raise tombstones with graves lined with straw.
Hide a rope on the step,
trip those candy swipers one at a time.
We laughed when they fell on their behinds.
Jump out of a tree on bended knee, dressed as a
werewolf howling at that girl.
Watched her and her friend take off and leave a pile of
smoke.
They thought it was no joke. We laughed as they ran, ran
ran.
They ran as fast as they could.
They ran down the street right through the neighborhood.
Once they got home, her dad called on the phone.
My brother the werewolf got his ass smacked
'Cause while she ran, she had an asthma attack.
Sad but true, now how about that?

<u>LOVE SPELL</u>

Snag six tiny wings from 3 different ladybugs
3 strands of ground up hair
from the one you're chasing for love
2 tablespoons of water charged by a full moon
add 1 tsp of graveyard dirt, use a silver spoon
stir until it becomes a thin paste
make sure none of it goes to waste
bury 3 feet under for 72 hours
this will increase its power
empty paste in a red pouch
add a letter to your love
draw stings, pull them tight
only at midnight mail the pouch
now wish upon a dove
you'll both soon be in love

MOTIONETTES

They are little motionettes,
they are spooky little plastics pets
they're little creepers whose eyes blink like peepers
I love them so much my little buddies
they scream wooooo high and scream wooooo low
their heads, back and forth, sway and roll
I love them to pieces
my little creatures their arms click and clatter
they're perfect, there is nothing the matter,
unless you drop them, they just might shatter
their jaws open, close and chatter
they hold brooms, skulls, chains and lanterns
they even rock in chairs, they spook up any room
they come with pumpkins, cauldrons and candles too
they sometimes even say BOO!
they kick their feet, they bow their heads,
gosh they're neat
they're something I truly adore,
I wish I had more more more

<u>FAR</u>

in the far you hear... a bark
in the far it's... silent
in the far you hear... a hoot
in the far it's... lonely
in the far you hear... crickets
in the far... it's dark
in the far you hear… nothing
in the far... is fear

VINTAGE

When I met you you were tall
When I met you you were red
When I met you you had a yellow head
When I met you you had a tail
When I met you you said noel
When I met you you plugged in
When I met you you lite the night
When I met you you cast a spell
When I met you you were my desire
When I met you you were made by Empire
Now all I think about are
your pumpkins, ghosts, witches and owls
As a kid you had a special place in my heart
I just loved how you spooked and lit the dark
To me you are my Halloween pals
To me I will always keep you in my memory

<u>ALL IN ONE NIGHT</u>

Halloween, that time of year.
You and me, don't have to be.
Grab a costume
throw it on
dunk for apples
sing a song
chilly night such a fright
fortune teller spooks the mind
no more candy left behind.

<u>NOT THE SAME!</u>

Trick-or-trunk SUCH A JOKE, what a snore!
There's nothing LIKE door to door
knock knock ding dong there's nothing more
than running house to house seeing what's in store.
Thank you Karens you short haired dorks!
That trick-or-trunk is such a bore
trick-or-trunk should be no more.
Who thought of that is not a sport.
Who thought of that we say NO MORE!
If we can't run the hood
you just never never understood
the thrill the feel the nightly chill
candy, costumes, friends and spooks
decorations on the roofs, decorations on the doors,
decorations in the yards but certainly not in or on the
cars!

<u>PRANKS</u>

Egg the windows,
toilet paper the trees.
Once you're found,
you'll beg them PLEASE...
NOT to throw you in the jail,
cause life there is pure fright,
especially on a Halloween night.

<u>GASP!</u>

I'm afraid of the dark, the moon,
mice and goons.
I don't wanna walk alone, hold my hand
don't make me ask you twice.
Now whistle a tune and please, please, please
tell me we'll be home very very soon.
Tonight the air is thin and
foggy this is what I dread,
listen to the froggies.
I've got to get out of my head.
I want to run, scream and holler.
I'm afraid of a monster.
I want this night to be over!
I'm holding for dear life to your collar.
I swear this is all a bad dream.
Home should not be much farther.

Fright Night

Tis the night witches, goons and
elves revel in fright.
Dancing and spooking all thru the night.
Tis the 'eve that mortals hide,
in hopes to miss.....
their horrid ride.

FAMILIAR

Oh my little imp my side by side familiar
how you know me as we are so similar
you never give up, go run nor hide
three hairs upon your head hide your eyes
piercing, deep and red
in the dark you are to dread
your two tiny toes and your pointy, thorn'd tail
you look like something straight from hell
your warts, crooked toes and skinny long nose
just make you the best, better than the rest
you know my thoughts, desires and needs
you're always there and aim to please
thank you from my stubborn, black heart
oh how I adore you
you're just so dang smart you stinky little fart
now hop in bed it's getting dark
tomorrow's a big day and we've an early start

VINTAGE CANDY

Butterfingers and Reeses,
Baby Ruths and Oh Henry!
Be good to your goblins…
Oh here they come, a loudly knockn'.

<u>TWAS THE NIGHT BEFORE HEXT-MAS</u>

'Twas the night before HEXT-mas, it was just me and my mouse.

We were putzing around the haunted old house.

The cobwebs were hung from the ceiling to scare in hopes that SATAN Nicolas wouldn't come near.

The Zombies were snug in their graves all dead,

with visions of ghosts and goblins for which all mortals do dread.

When all of a sudden there arose such a splatter, I sprang from my bed and tripped over a cadaver.

I threw open the broken shutters, to see what was up

and there was a shadow, a scary old figure.

He was slumped over, for I thought he was drunk.

I yelled to see if it was my neighbor, cause he is a jerk... I owe him a favor.

As he cursed at his minions, one at a time, yelling their names, smasher and spider, pumpkin and gore...

Shhh, quiet before we blow it!

Hanukkah will be here before you know it.

Now slash away, slash away, slash away all.

Those demons, they stood on my rotting roof, pawing and clawing each tiny horned hoof.

This peddler, snuck down my chimney covered in soot.

He was dressed like an evil old elf.

A blunt pipe he clinched in his teeth.

His cheeks were blood red and he smelled like a thief.

He opened his bag and stole all I had.

He then turned with a jerk and gave me the finger.

Then out the broken window he sprang like a flash.

He tore his pants, I know, I saw his skinny ass.

He unzipped his drawers and pissed on my grass.

Then jumped in his hearse and continued to curse.

In spite of myself, I started to giggle.

The only thing he left was a burnt old log, too small for a fire but perfect for a frog.

And I heard him claim as he skidded off....

"Thanks for the Rum Chata you ugly old hag!

Go to bed, for you have lots to fear.

Until then, hope I don't see you next year!"

ABOUT THE AUTHOR

BORAH! Brewington Snaggletooth XIII lives alone far, far, deep in a cold, thick, wet, foggy forest hidden deep on the edge of Salem, MA. They are a stanky, miserable, quick witted, sassy 400 plus year old witch.

BORAH! is not too fond of being around you mortals however has a fondness for little children and is always looking for the right one to throw in their cauldron along with some carrots, celery and potatoes, unwashed and covered with dirt of course.

There's not too many things BORAH! loves. But for sure, BORAH! loves to street perform, LOVES Halloween and LOVES Salem, MA... put all three together and BORAH! gives you ONE WICKED good time!

In addition to street performing, BORAH! officiates weddings around the US, they also renew wedding vows and gender reveals. BORAH! gives back to the community of Salem by donating to a different charity each year. BORAH! has appeared in numerous tv shows and news articles around the world.

Everyone kept asking BORAH! to write a book. So the old hag sat down one rainy night and penned this book of poems which were all inspired from their childhood memories. BORAH! hopes this pitiful book of poems and pictures takes you back to your horrible childhood and brings you horrific memories, forced laughs, maybe a screech and a tear or two.

Continue to decorate more and more and celebrate your love for Halloween and spread yucky, Halloween cheer, never be embarrassed of your passion for horror, Halloween or being different.

Feed all those kiddies sugar filled candies and do, DO scare the living daylights out of them please.

Happy Halloween and hope you hate it. BORAH!

ABOUT THE ILLUSTRATOR

As an artist Halloween has always found a way to creep into my work. I very much enjoy the creative process, conjuring life into my creations utilizing all types of media. I hope you enjoy my contributions here and they inspire some wonderful memories of Halloween for you. Thank you so much Borah for believing in my work....I hate you.

Made in the USA
Middletown, DE
03 September 2023